CAMBRIDGE PRIMARY
Science

Skills Builder

Fiona Baxter and Liz Dilley

CAMBRIDGE
UNIVERSITY PRESS

CAMBRIDGE UNIVERSITY PRESS

University Printing House, Cambridge CB2 8BS, United Kingdom

One Liberty Plaza, 20th Floor, New York, NY 10006, USA

477 Williamstown Road, Port Melbourne, VIC 3207, Australia

4843/24, 2nd Floor, Ansari Road, Daryaganj, Delhi – 110002, India

103 Penang Road, #05-06/07, Visioncrest Commercial, Singapore 238467

Cambridge University Press is part of the University of Cambridge.

It furthers the University's mission by disseminating knowledge in the pursuit of education, learning and research at the highest international levels of excellence.

Information on this title: education.cambridge.org

© Cambridge University Press 2016

This publication is in copyright. Subject to statutory exception and to the provisions of relevant collective licensing agreements, no reproduction of any part may take place without the written permission of Cambridge University Press.

First published 2016

20 19 18 17 16 15 14 13 12 11 10

Produced for Cambridge University Press by
White-Thomson Publishing
www.wtpub.co.uk

Editor: Sonya Newland
Designer: Tracey Camden

Printed in Italy by Rotolito S.p.A.

A catalogue record for this publication is available from the British Library

ISBN 978-1-316-61106-7 Paperback

Additional resources for this publication at www.cambridge.org/

Cambridge University Press has no responsibility for the persistence or accuracy of URLs for external or third-party internet websites referred to in this publication, and does not guarantee that any content on such websites is, or will remain, accurate or appropriate. Information regarding prices, travel timetables, and other factual information given in this work is correct at the time of first printing but Cambridge University Press does not guarantee the accuracy of such information thereafter.

NOTICE TO TEACHERS IN THE UK
It is illegal to reproduce any part of this work in material form (including photocopying and electronic storage) except under the following circumstances:
(i) where you are abiding by a licence granted to your school or institution by the Copyright Licensing Agency;
(ii) where no such licence exists, or where you wish to exceed the terms of a licence, and you have gained the written permission of Cambridge University Press;
(iii) where you are allowed to reproduce without permission under the provisions of Chapter 3 of the Copyright, Designs and Patents Act 1988, which covers, for example, the reproduction of short passages within certain types of educational anthology and reproduction for the purposes of setting examination questions.

Contents

Introduction		**4**
1	**Investigating plant growth**	**5**
1.3	Investigating germination	6
1.4	What do plants need to grow?	8
2	**The life cycle of flowering plants**	**9**
2.1	Why plants have flowers	10
2.2	How seeds are spread	12
2.4	The parts of a flower	14
2.5	Pollination	16
2.6	Investigating pollination	18
2.7	Plant life cycles	20
3	**States of matter**	**22**
3.1	Evaporation	23
3.2	Why evaporation is useful	24
3.3	Investigating evaporation	25
3.4	Solutions and evaporation	27
3.5	Condensation	28
3.6	The water cycle	29
3.8	Melting	32
3.9	Measuring temperature	34
4	**The way we see things**	**36**
4.1	Light travels from a source	37
4.3	Seeing behind you	39
4.4	Which surfaces reflect light best?	41
5	**Shadows**	**43**
5.1	Light travels in straight lines	44
5.2	Which materials let light through?	46
5.3	Silhouettes and shadow puppets	48
5.4	What affects the size of a shadow?	50
5.5	Investigating shadow lengths	51
5.6	Measuring light intensity	52
6	**Earth's movements**	**53**
6.1	The Sun, the Earth and the Moon	54
6.2	Does the Sun move?	55
6.3	The Earth rotates on its axis	57
6.5	The Earth revolves around the Sun	58
6.6	Exploring the solar system	60
Answers		**63**
Glossary		**70**

Introduction

This series of primary science activity books complements *Cambridge Primary Science* and promotes, through practice, learner confidence and depth of knowledge in the skills of scientific enquiry (SE) and key scientific vocabulary and concepts. These activity books will:

- enhance and extend learners' scientific knowledge and facts
- promote scientific enquiry skills and learning in order to think like a scientist
- advance each learner's knowledge and use of scientific vocabulary and concepts in their correct context.

The *Skills Builders* activity books consolidate core topics that learners have *already* covered in the classroom, providing those learners with that extra reinforcement of SE skills, vocabulary topic knowledge and understanding. They have been written with a focus on scientific literacy with ESL/EAL learners in mind.

How to use the activity books

These activity books have been designed for use by individual learners, either in the classroom or at home. As teachers and as parents, you can decide how and when they are used by your learner to best improve their progress. The *Skills Builder* activity books target specific topics (lessons) from Grades 1–6 from all the units covered in *Cambridge Primary Science*. This targeted approach has been carefully designed to consolidate topics where it is most needed.

How to use the units

Unit introduction

Each unit starts with an introduction for you as the teacher or parent. It clearly sets out which topics are covered in the unit and the learning objectives of the activities in each section. This is where you can work with learners to select all, most or just one of the sections according to individual needs.

The introduction also provides advice and tips on how best to support the learner in the skills of scientific enquiry and in the practice of key scientific vocabulary.

Sections

Each section matches a corresponding lesson in the main series. Sections contain write-in activities that are supported by:

- Key words – key vocabulary for the topic, also highlighted in bold in the sections
- Key facts – a short fact to support the activities where relevant
- Look and learn – where needed, activities are supported with scientific exemplars for extra support of how to treat a concept or scientific method
- Remember – tips for the learner to steer them in the right direction.

How to approach the write-in activities

Teachers and parents are advised to provide students with a blank A5 notebook at the start of each grade for learners to use alongside these activity books. Most activities will provide enough space for the answers required. However, some learner responses – especially to enquiry-type questions – may require more space for notes. Keeping notes and plans models how scientists work and encourages learners to explore and record their thinking, leaving the activity books for the final, more focused answers.

Think about it questions

Each unit also contains some questions for discussion at home with parents, or at school. Although learners will record the outcomes of their discussions in the activity book, these questions are intended to encourage the students to think more deeply.

Self-assessment

Each section in the unit ends with a self-assessment opportunity for learners: empty circles with short learning statements. Teachers or parents can ask learners to complete the circles in a number of ways, depending on their age and preference, e.g. with faces, traffic light colours or numbers. The completed self-assessments provide teachers with a clearer understanding of how best to progress and support individual learners.

Glossary of key words and concepts

At the end of each activity book there is a glossary of key scientific words and concepts arranged by unit. Learners are regularly reminded to practise saying these words out loud and in sentences to improve communication skills in scientific literacy.

1. Investigating plant growth

What learners will practise and reinforce

The activities in this Skills Builder unit give learners further practice in the following topics in the Learner's Book and Activity Book:

Topic	In this topic, learners will:
1.3 Investigating germination	draw a bar chart to show the results of an investigation into seed germination
1.4 What do plants need to grow?	identify the factors that plants need for growth
1.5 Plants and light	see Challenge, Section 1.5

Help your learner

In this unit, learners will practise presenting results in a bar chart and recognising patterns in data (Section 1.3). To help them:

1 Ask learners to look carefully at the data in the table in Section 1.3 before drawing the bar chart. They will need to draw a bar for each type of seed after five days and after ten days.

2 Germinate a few seeds and let learners observe the stages of germination to reinforce what they have learnt in class. Smaller seeds such as radishes and chillies usually germinate more quickly, but if you germinate seeds such as lentils, you can eat the sprouts.

TEACHING TIP

Remind learners to look at the information provided about the investigation in Section 1.3. Were the seeds different in any way? Can they see a pattern in the results related to this?

1.3 Investigating germination

seeds, germinate

Draw a chart of seed germination

Ella and her friends planted some **seeds** in pots of soil to **germinate**. They put the pots in a warm place and watered them every day. They noted the results after five days and ten days. These are their results:

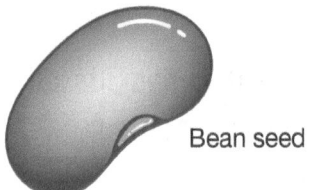
Bean seed

Chilli seed

Sunflower seed

Type of seed	Number of seeds germinated after five days	Number of seeds germinated after ten days
bean	0	3
chilli	5	12
sunflower	3	7

1 Draw a bar chart of the results shown in the table.

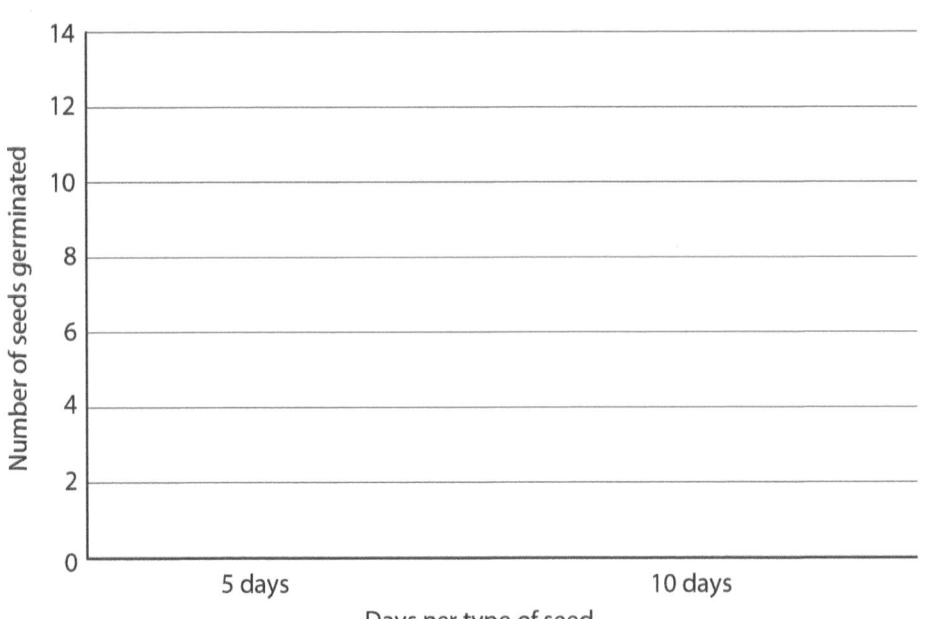

Remember:

In a bar chart, the bars must be separate because each bar shows a different group or object – for example the type of seed.

2 a Do seeds need light to germinate? Explain the evidence for your answer from Ella's investigation.

_____

_____

_____

b Name two things that Ella and her friends did to make sure that the seeds germinated.

_____

_____

3 Which seeds germinated fastest?

_____

4 Which seeds germinated slowest?

_____

5 What pattern can you see in the results?

_____

_____

_____

_____

CHECK YOUR LEARNING

○ I can draw a bar chart and find patterns in the results.

○ I can identify factors that seeds need to germinate.

1.4 What do plants need to grow?

factors

Identify the things that plants need to grow

1 Look at these sentences about the things that plants need to grow. Fill in the gaps using words from the box.

> light   water   air   warmth   **factors**

a   We call the things that plants need to grow _____ .

b   Plants need _____ so they can make food to help them grow.

c   Plants need _____ to give them strong stems and firm leaves.

d   Plants need _____ , but they grow best when it is not too cold or too hot.

e   Plants need _____ because they are living things.

2 Think about it!

Why do plants need light to grow, but seeds do not need light to germinate?

_____

_____

CHECK YOUR LEARNING

◯   I can identify the things that plants need to grow.

2 The life cycle of flowering plants

What learners will practise and reinforce

The activities in this Skills Builder unit give learners further practice in the following topics in the Learner's Book and Activity Book:

Topic	In this topic, learners will:
2.1 Why plants have flowers	record information about flowers in a table, draw a bar chart and explain why flowers are important
2.2 How seeds are spread	explain how seeds are suited to the way they are spread
2.3 Other ways seeds are spread	see Challenge, Section 2.3
2.4 The parts of a flower	identify and describe the different parts of a flower
2.5 Pollination	understand pollination and fertilisation
2.6 Investigating pollination	analyse results about pollinators and draw a bar chart
2.7 Plant life cycles	complete a crossword puzzle on pollination

Help your learner

In this unit, learners will practise presenting results in bar charts (Sections 2.1 and 2.6) and interpreting data and thinking about whether it is sufficient to draw conclusions (Section 2.6). To help them:

1 Talk about the importance of making sure there is enough evidence to form a conclusion. Explain that the best way to do this is by repeating the investigation a few times, as scientists do.

> **TEACHING TIP**
>
> Try to make this unit as practical as possible by observing seeds, flowers and pollinators if you can.

2.1 Why plants have flowers

scent

LOOK AND LEARN

Most (but not all) plants have flowers. When the flowers die, part of them remains on the plant and becomes the fruit. This is why you do not often see fruit and flowers on a plant at the same time – they are different stages in the plant's life cycle.

Draw a bar chart of different flowers

Dineo and Jojo visited a garden. They saw 10 big flowers, 16 small flowers, 5 flowers with **scent** and 9 flowers with no scent.

1 Record Dineo and Jojo's observations in the table.

Remember:

Think about the headings you will use for each column of the table.

2 Draw a bar chart of the results.

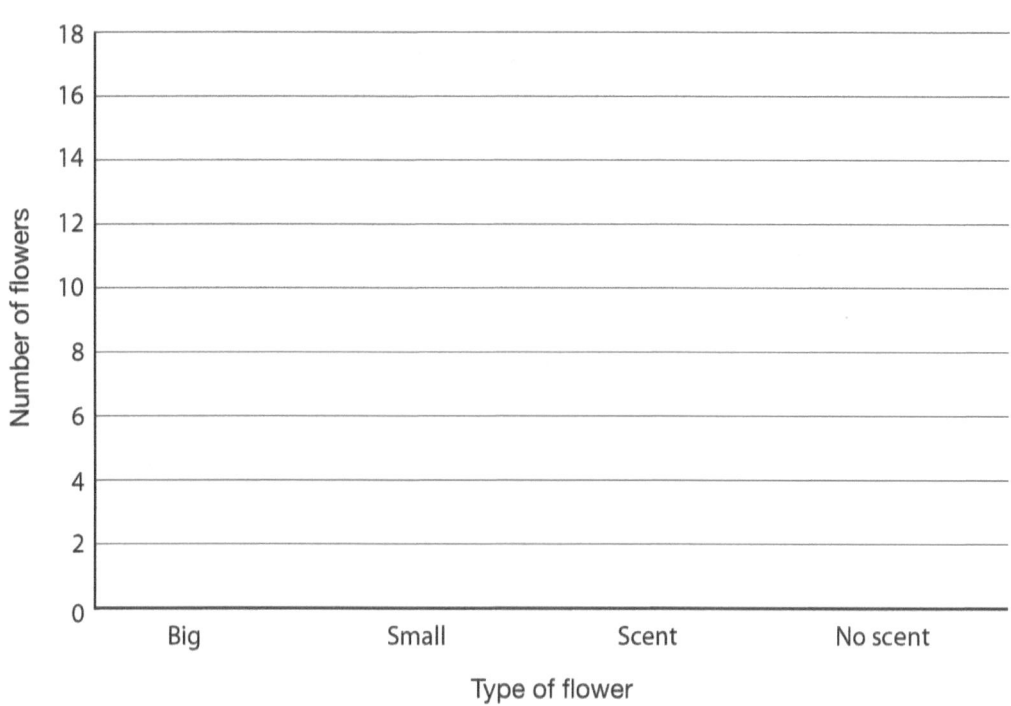

3 Explain why flowers are important to plants.

_____

_____

_____

CHECK YOUR LEARNING

◯ I can fill in a table of results.

◯ I can draw a bar chart.

◯ I can explain why flowers are important.

2.2 How seeds are spread

> dispersal

Explain how seeds suit the way they are spread

1 Match the way seeds and fruit are spread to the description of the seed. Draw a line from the first column to the correct answer in the second column.

by water	seed has spines and hooks
by air	seed pods dry out and burst open
by animals	fruit is heavy and drops to the ground
by gravity	seed has spongy covering that helps it float
by explosion	seed is very light with thin, papery wings

2 What do we call the spreading of seeds away from the parent plant?

_____

3 Why is it important for seeds to be spread?

_____

_____

_____

CHECK YOUR LEARNING

○ I can identify how seeds and fruits are suited to the way they are spread.

○ I can explain why seeds must be spread.

2.4 The parts of a flower

sepals, petals, anther, stamen, stigma, ovary, pollen

Identify and describe parts of a flower

1. Colour in the different parts of the flower. Use these colours:

   green – **sepals**

   blue – **petals**

   orange – **anther**

   black – **stamen**

   yellow – **stigma**

   brown – **ovary**

Remember: Practise saying these words aloud. Try to use them when talking about the topic.

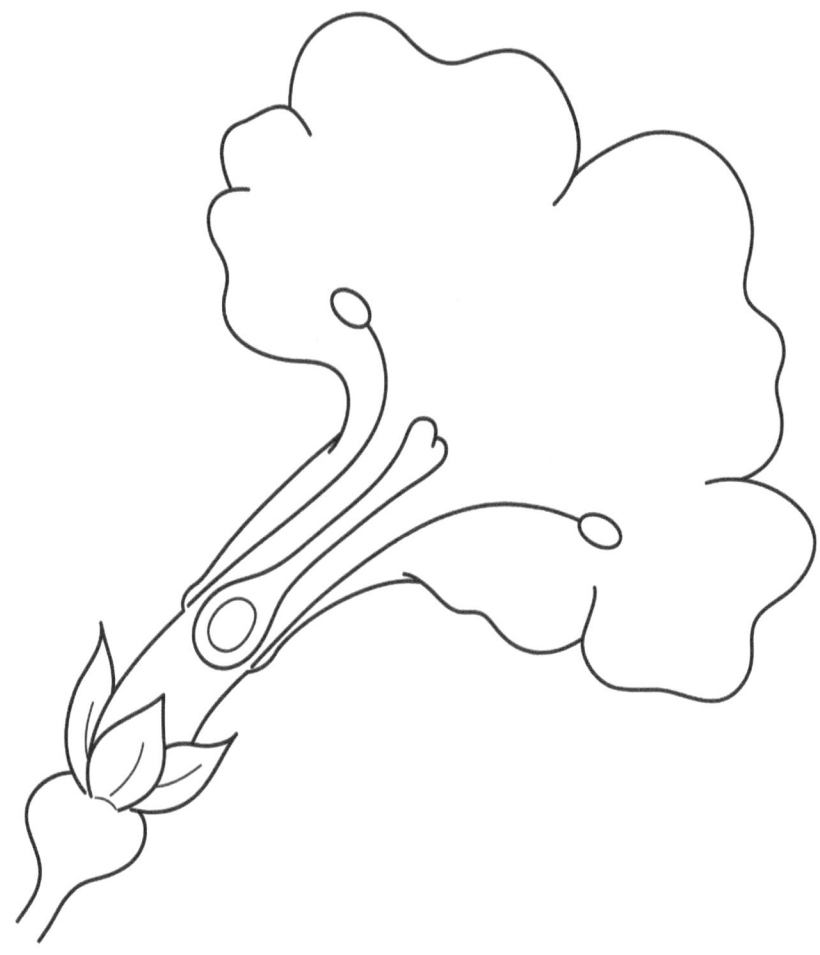

2 Look at these sentences describing what the different parts of a flower do. Use the words in the box to fill in the spaces below.

> stigma   sepals   ovary   petals   anthers   stamens

The _____ are little green leaves that protect the flower bud. The _____ often have bright colours to attract insects. The male parts of the flower are the _____. They make **pollen** in their tips, called _____. The female part of the flower is made up of the _____, which collects pollen, and the _____, which contains the eggs.

CHECK YOUR LEARNING

○ I can identify different parts of a flower.

○ I can explain what different parts of a flower do.

2.5 Pollination

pollination, fertilisation

Answer questions about pollination and fertilisation

Underline the correct answer to complete these statements.

1 Pollen moves from the stamen to the stigma in a process called ...
  a dispersal
  b **pollination**
  c germination
  d fertilisation.

2 Flowers pollinated by insects have ...
  a big stigmas
  b bright colours
  c no scent
  d no petals.

3 The process that takes place when the pollen and egg join in the ovary is called ...
  a dispersal
  b pollination
  c germination
  d fertilisation.

4 The part of the flower that forms the fruit is called the ...
  a ovary
  b petal
  c sepal
  d stamen.

5 Think about it!

The flowers in the drawings only have male or female parts. Describe the process of pollination in flowers like these.

_____

_____

_____

_____

_____

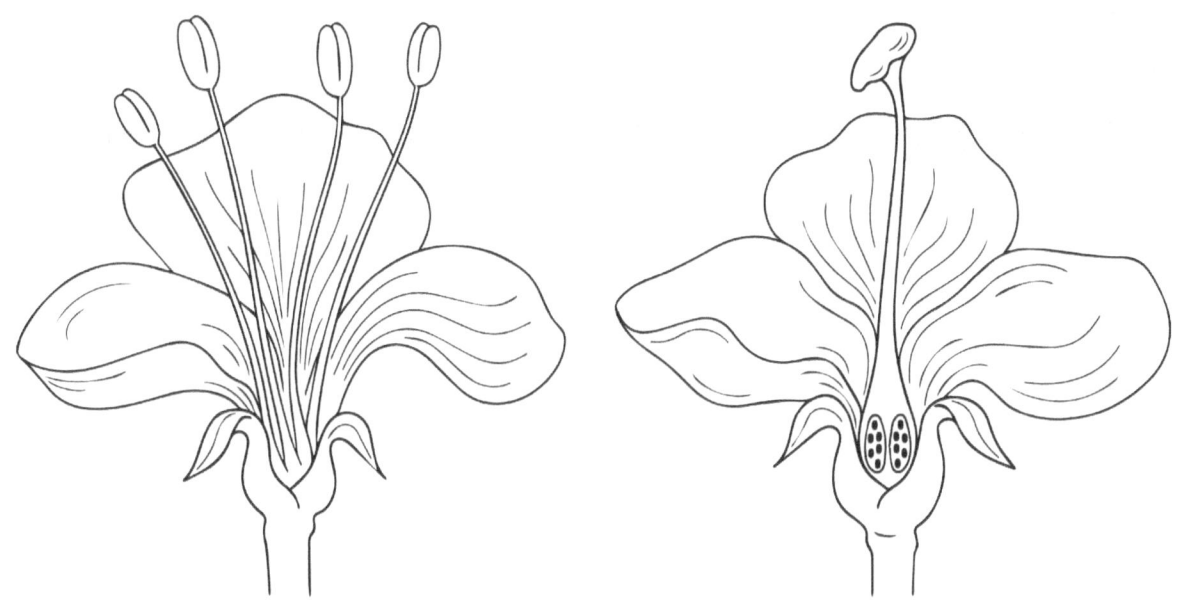

CHECK YOUR LEARNING

○ I know about pollination and fertilisation in plants.

2.6 Investigating pollination

pollinator, style

Identify which colour flowers insects visit most

Aliyah's class observed and counted insects visiting different coloured flowers. These are their results:

Colour of flower	Number of insects that visited flower
red	3
yellow	12
white	10
blue	6

1 Draw a bar chart of the results. Use a different colour for each bar.

Flower colour

2 a Which colour flower did the most insects visit?

_____

b Which colour flower did the fewest insects visit? Suggest a reason for this.

_____

_____

3 a What conclusion can you draw from the results?

_____

_____

b What can you do to be sure your conclusion is correct?

_____

> ### KEY FACT
>
> During pollination, a **pollinator** brings pollen from the male stamen of a flower to the female stigma. The pollen moves from the stigma down a hollow tube called the **style** until it gets to the ovary. There are eggs in the ovary. Fertilisation happens when the pollen and eggs join.

CHECK YOUR LEARNING

◯ I can draw a bar chart.

◯ I can interpret results.

◯ I can decide whether there is enough data to form a conclusion.

2 The life cycle of flowering plants

2.7 Plant life cycles

Complete a crossword puzzle

Follow the clues to complete the crossword puzzle on plant life cycles. Choose your answers from the words in the box.

| germination | seeds | fruit | flowering | growth | anthers |
| pollinator | pollination | dispersal | fertilisation | | |

Across

3 This happens when the pollen and egg join.

5 They form from the fertilised egg.

8 They produce pollen.

9 This happens when the pollen lands on the stigma.

10 The way a young plant gets bigger.

Down

1 This happens when the plant is ready to reproduce.

2 This happens when the seed starts to grow.

4 It contains the seeds.

6 The process by which seeds are spread.

7 It carries pollen from flower to flower.

CHECK YOUR LEARNING

○ I know about the stages in the life cycle of a plant.

2 The life cycle of flowering plants

3 States of matter

What learners will practise and reinforce

The activities in this Skills Builder unit give learners further practice in the following topics in the Learner's Book and Activity Book:

Topic	In this topic, learners will:
3.1 Evaporation	identify correct and incorrect statements about evaporation
3.2 Why evaporation is useful	draw a line graph of results and make a prediction
3.3 Investigating evaporation	draw a graph and recognise factors that affect evaporation
3.4 Solutions and evaporation	identify true and false statements
3.5 Condensation	complete sentences about condensation
3.6 The water cycle	explain the changes of state in the water cycle
3.7 Boiling	see Challenge, Section 3.7
3.8 Melting	identify correct and incorrect statements about melting
3.9 Measuring temperature	explain how to measure temperature and read a diagram of a thermometer

Help your learner

In this unit, learners will practise presenting results in line graphs, making predictions of what will happen and using knowledge and understanding to plan a fair test (Section 3.3). To help them:

1 Remind learners that we use a line graph to show how something changes with time, such as the amount of water in a container. Line graphs always have numbers on both axes. Learners should plot the data points first and then join them neatly with a pencil.

TEACHING TIP

Evaporation happens all around us, every day. Point out examples in daily life to learners.

3.1 Evaporation

evaporation

LOOK AND LEARN

If water is heated up, its particles gain energy. They begin moving faster, which makes them bump into each other and transfer energy. Eventually, some particles will have so much energy that they will break free from the surface of the water. We say that the particles have evaporated.

Evaporation true or false

Look at these statements about **evaporation**. Mark each one as either true (✓) or false (✗).

- [ ] **1** Evaporation occurs when a liquid changes to a gas.
- [ ] **2** Heat makes evaporation happen faster.
- [ ] **3** Particles of a liquid must lose energy before they can evaporate.
- [ ] **4** Evaporation makes wet clothes dry.
- [ ] **5** Water disappears when it evaporates.

CHECK YOUR LEARNING

○ I can identify true and false statements about evaporation.

KEY FACT

In the water cycle, water changes state from liquid to gas when it evaporates. It condenses back into a liquid to form clouds. Water can also freeze and become a solid, such as hail or snow.

3.2 Why evaporation is useful

factors

Explain how evaporation dries things

Ming and Kumei are going to a party. Ten minutes before they are going to leave, Ming spills a glass of water down the front of her dress.

1 What can Kumei do to help Ming dry her dress in time for the party?

_____

2 Explain how evaporation makes the dress dry.

_____

_____

3 Name two **factors** that might help to speed up the process.

_____

4 Name two other ways that evaporation is useful to us.

_____

_____

CHECK YOUR LEARNING

○ I can explain how evaporation makes things dry.

○ I can name two uses of evaporation.

Remember:
Evaporation is when liquid particles gain heat energy and turn into a gas.

3.3 Investigating evaporation

Draw a graph of factors that affect evaporation

Akia and Dembe investigated the factors that affect the evaporation of water. They placed one bowl of water in a warm place and another bowl of water in a cool place.

These are their results:

Day	Volume of water in bowl (ml)	
	Warm place	Cool place
1	250	250
2	200	230
3	150	210
4	90	180
5	50	150

Remember:

Water needs energy in order to evaporate and change from a liquid to a gas.

1 Draw a graph showing the results for each bowl of water.

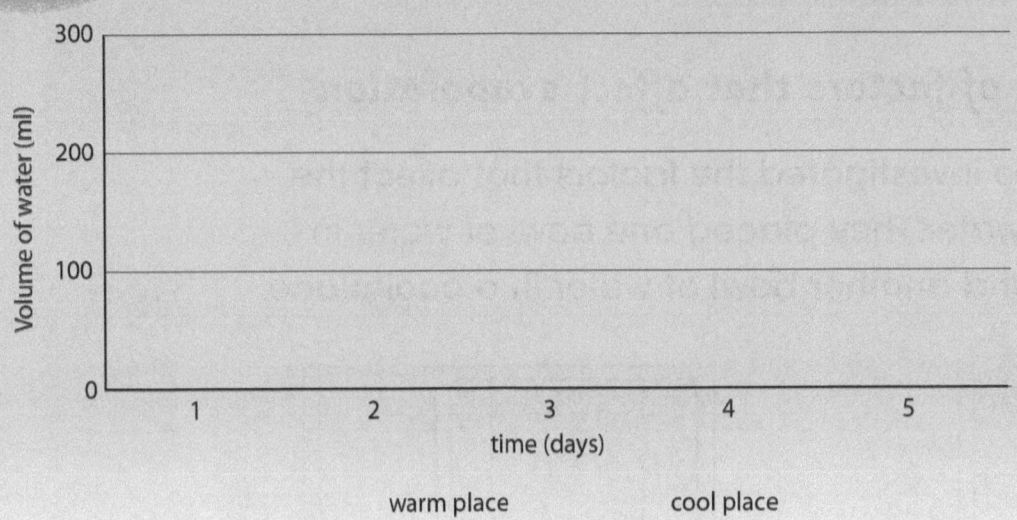

2 a In which bowl did most evaporation take place? State the evidence for your answer.

_____

_____

b Which factor affected the amount of water that evaporated?

_____

3 Was this a fair test? Say why or why not.

_____

_____

CHECK YOUR LEARNING

◯ I can choose the right type of graph to draw and record my results.

◯ I can use my knowledge about evaporation to make a prediction.

◯ I can recognise a fair test.

3.4 Solutions and evaporation

solutions

Solutions true or false

Read these statements about **solutions** and evaporation. Mark each one as either true (✓) or false (✗).

☐ **1** A solution is made of a solute and solvent.

☐ **2** The solvent dissolves in the solute to form a solution.

☐ **3** We cannot see the solute particles in a solution.

☐ **4** We can separate the solute and solvent in a solution by evaporation.

☐ **5** The water that evaporates from a salt solution will taste salty.

CHECK YOUR LEARNING

○ I know that when a liquid evaporates from a solution, the solid is left behind.

3.5 Condensation

condensation, water vapour

Complete sentences about condensation

Choose words from the box to complete the sentences about **condensation**. You will not need to use all the words.

| solid | gas | liquid | gain | lose | cool down | heat up |
| melting | evaporation | drops | drops | warmer | cooler |

1 Condensation happens when a _____ changes to a _____.

2 We know that condensation has happened when we see _____ of water on a surface.

3 Condensation happens when **water vapour** touches a _____ surface. This makes the particles of water vapour _____ and _____ energy.

4 The opposite process to condensation is _____.

CHECK YOUR LEARNING

○ I can explain how condensation happens.

28 3.5 Condensation

3.6 The water cycle

water cycle

Explain the water cycle

Look at the diagram of the **water cycle**.

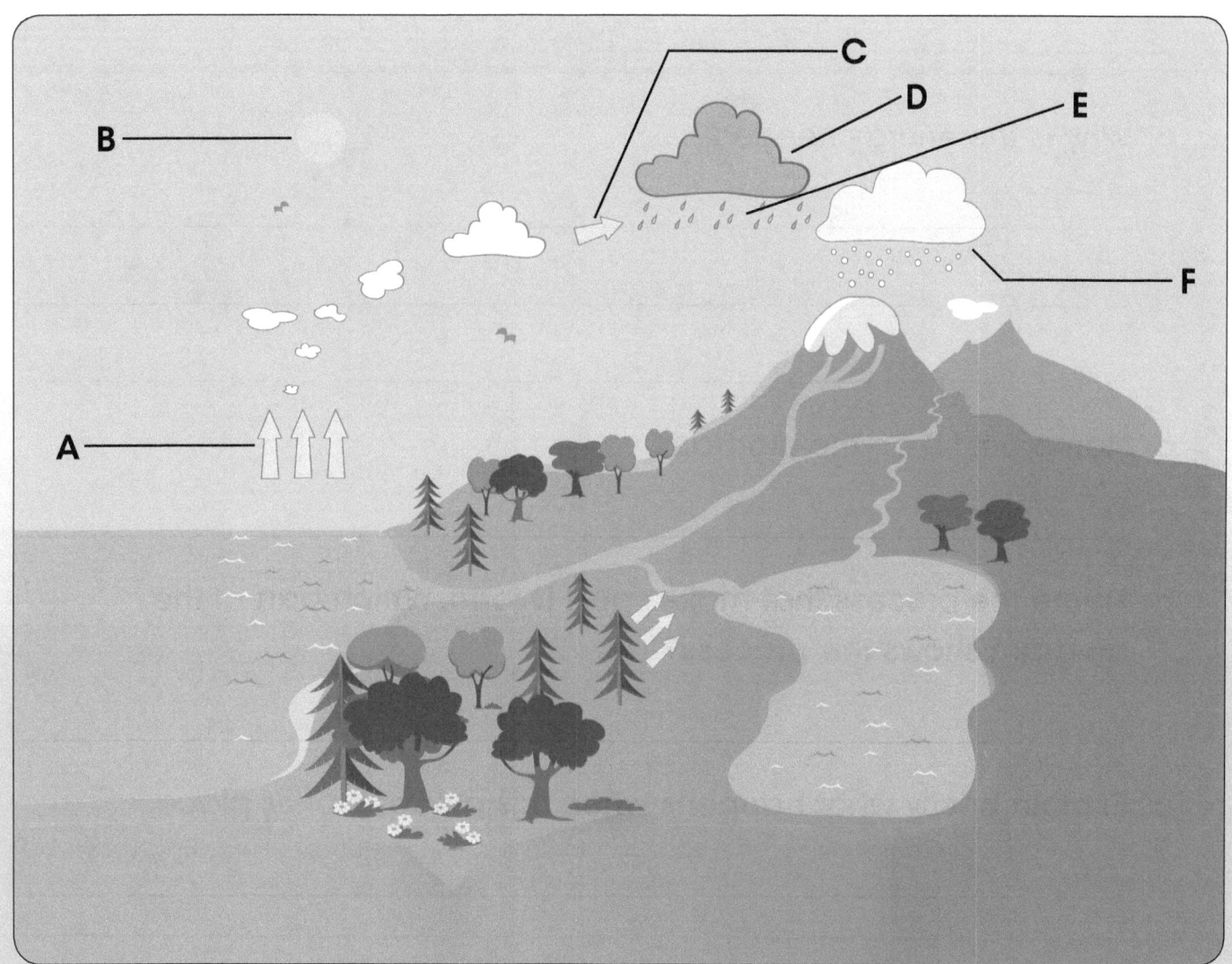

1 a Name the process that takes place at A on the diagram.

_____

b Which letter on the diagram shows the source of energy for this process?

_____

c Why is the energy needed?

_____

_____

2 a Name part D on the diagram.

_____

b Name the process that makes part D form. Which part of the diagram shows this process?

_____

c Explain briefly what happens when this process takes place.

_____

_____

_____

3 a Name the substance labelled E.

_____

b Is this substance a solid, liquid or gas?

_____

c Name another state in which this substance can fall to Earth. Which part of the diagram shows this happening?

_____

4 Think about it!

Why is there no rain in Antarctica?

_____

_____

_____

_____

CHECK YOUR LEARNING

◯ I can identify the changes of the state of water in the water cycle.

◯ I can explain why energy is needed in the water cycle.

3.8 Melting

melting, melting points, particles

Melting multiple choice

Underline the correct answer to each question.

1 When ice cream becomes liquid on a hot day it is …

    a freezing

    b melting

    c condensing

    d cooling.

2 We can show the process of **melting** like this:

    a liquid + heat → solid

    b gas − heat → liquid

    c solid + heat → liquid

    d solid − heat → liquid.

> **KEY FACT**
>
> Just as different liquids have different boiling points, different solids have different **melting points**. The melting point of some metals, for example, is very high. The melting point of ice is low — only 0 °C.

3 We can show the process of freezing like this:

    a liquid − heat → solid

    b gas + heat → liquid

    c solid + heat → liquid

    d gas − heat → solid.

4 Solids melt because …

    a their **particles** gain energy and break away from the solid

    b their particles are not moving fast enough to stay in the solid

    c new liquid particles form when the solid is heated

    d solids cannot keep their shape when heated.

5 The opposite of ice melting is water …

    a condensing

    b thawing

    c cooling

    d freezing.

CHECK YOUR LEARNING

○   I know about the process of melting.

3.9 Measuring temperature

> thermometers, expands, contracts, temperature

LOOK AND LEARN

Thermometers are filled with a liquid. This liquid **expands** and takes up more space when it is heated. It **contracts** and takes up less space when it cools. An increase in **temperature** makes the liquid expand and rise in the glass tube of the thermometer. When the liquid cools, it contracts and drops back down the glass tube.

Measuring temperature with a thermometer

1 Underline the correct word or words in each sentence to make the sentence true.

   a Always hold the *top* / *bulb* of the thermometer.

   b Make sure your eye is *above* / *level* with the top of the liquid in the thermometer.

   c When you measure the temperature of liquids, make sure *most* / *all* of the bulb is in the liquid.

   d Read the temperature scale *before* / *after* the thermometer reading stops changing.

   e Read the temperature scale *before* / *after* you take the thermometer out of the liquid.

2 Look at the drawing of the thermometer.

   a Write down the temperature reading on the thermometer.

   b Mark the boiling point of water on the thermometer.

   c Mark the melting point of ice on the thermometer.

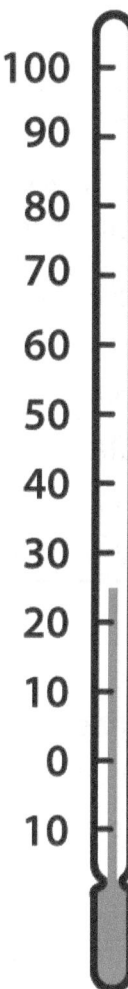

CHECK YOUR LEARNING

○ I can identify true and false statements about measuring temperature with a thermometer.

○ I can read and mark temperatures on a thermometer.

4 The way we see things

What learners will practise and reinforce

The activities in this Skills Builder unit give learners further practice in the following topics in the Learner's Book and Activity Book:

Topic	In this topic, learners will:
4.1 Light travels from a source	know that light travels from a source and reflects off objects into our eyes
4.2 Mirrors	see Challenge, Section 4.2
4.3 Seeing behind you	discover how mirrors can help you to see behind you
4.4 Which surfaces reflect light best?	investigate surfaces that reflect and absorb light
4.5 Light changes direction	See Challenge, Section 4.5

Help your learner

In this unit, learners will practise making relevant observations from pictures and diagrams (Sections 4.1 and 4.3). They will also practise making predictions based on their scientific knowledge (Sections 4.1 and 4.3). To help them:

1 Encourage learners to experiment with mirrors to help them understand all the necessary concepts.

2 Ask learners to tell you how they see things on the table or outside. Each time, they should remember that the light comes from a light source to an object and then into their eyes.

TEACHING TIP

Have some small mirrors available to help learners with the activities. Make sure the mirrors have bound edges to avoid the risk of learners cutting themselves.

4.1 Light travels from a source

light source, object

Describe how we see objects

Mrs Liong is doing some sewing. She needs to see the needle she is trying to thread.

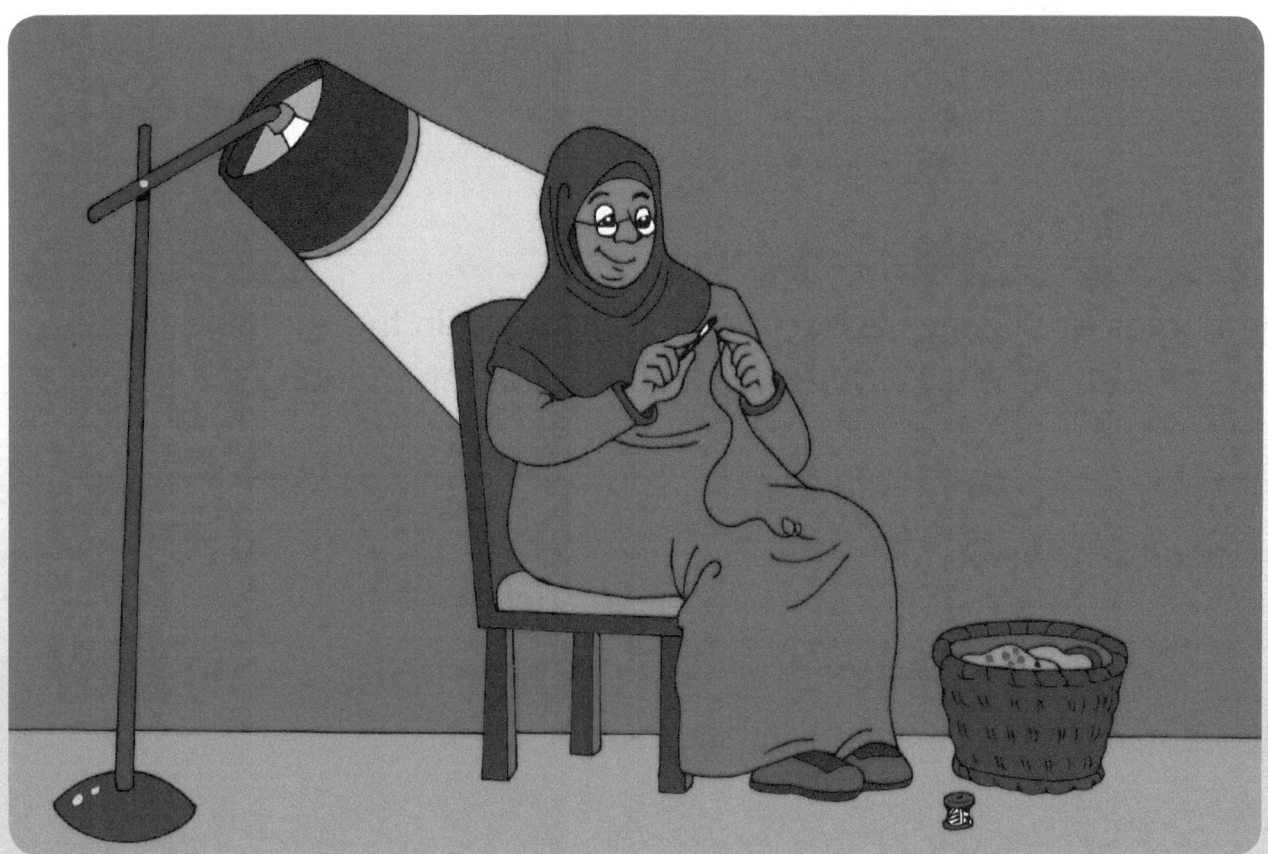

1 Name the **light source** Mrs Liong is using.

_____

KEY FACT

Light travels from a source to an **object**.
The light is reflected off the object into our eyes.

2 Name the object Mrs Liong is trying to see.

_____

3 On the picture, draw lines with arrows to show how Mrs Liong sees the object.

> **Remember:**
>
> When showing how light travels on a diagram, use straight lines and use arrows to show the direction that light is travelling in.

4 Sometimes Mrs Liong sits outside in her garden in the morning and sews. What light source does Mrs Liong use in the morning?

_____

CHECK YOUR LEARNING

○ I know that light travels from a source.

○ I can name some different light sources.

4.3 Seeing behind you

mirror, image, surface, reflects

LOOK AND LEARN

When you look at yourself in a **mirror**, you are looking at the light from your face reflecting off the surface of the mirror, which travels to your eyes. Mirrors reflect light well because they are smooth, polished surfaces.

Remember:

Practise saying these words aloud. Try to use them when talking about the topic.

Explain how to use a mirror to see behind you

Adeline is sitting in the chair looking into a mirror. Thandi is standing behind her, holding another mirror. She has just finished braiding Adeline's hair.

1 Look at the description of how Adeline sees the back of her head. Choose words from the box to complete the sentences. You will need to use some words more than once.

> image   mirror   surface   reflects   in front

Adeline is looking at a _____. She can see the _____ of her face. This is because the _____ has a smooth, shiny _____. It _____ light well. Thandi is holding a second _____. Adeline can see the _____ of the back of her head in the mirror _____ of her.

2 On the picture, draw lines to show how light reflects off the mirrors so that Adeline can see the back of her head. Label one of the lines you draw 'light from source'. Show the direction the light travels with arrows.

3 Think about it!

Name one natural light source and one artificial light source that you use every day.

_____

_____

CHECK YOUR LEARNING

○ I understand how you can use mirrors to see behind you.

○ I can show the way light travels on a picture.

4.3 Seeing behind you

4.4 Which surfaces reflect light best?

absorb

Compare how well two surfaces reflect light

LOOK AND LEARN

All objects either reflect or **absorb** light. The amount of light reflected depends on the surface of the object. To reflect light, a surface must be very smooth. Bumpy surfaces will absorb more light than they reflect.

Resources
You will need a torch with a strong beam and two objects. Choose one object that you think will reflect light well and one object you think will absorb light.

1 Write down the two objects you have chosen and the materials they are made from.

_____

_____

2 Plan a fair test to investigate your prediction of which object will reflect light well and which will absorb light. Describe how you will make the test fair.

_____

_____

_____

_____

4 The way we see things

3 Carry out your investigation. Were your results what you predicted?

_____

4 What do you conclude about which surfaces reflect light and which surfaces absorb light?

_____

_____

_____

5 What can you do to collect more data to confirm your conclusion?

_____

_____

CHECK YOUR LEARNING

○ I can conduct a fair test.

○ I know which surfaces reflect light well and which surfaces absorb light.

5 Shadows

What learners will practise and reinforce

The activities in this Skills Builder unit give learners further practice in the following topics in the Learner's Book and Activity Book:

Topic	In this topic, learners will:
5.1 Light travels in straight lines	explain how shadows form
5.2 Which materials let light through?	discover that opaque, translucent and transparent materials let through different amounts of light
5.3 Silhouettes and shadow puppets	see how a shadow puppet works
5.4 What affects the size of a shadow?	discover that the size of a shadow is affected by the position of the puppet
5.5 Investigating shadow lengths	understand that shadows change in length and position throughout the day
5.6 Measuring light intensity	explain light intensity
5.7 How scientists measured and understood light	see Challenge, Section 5.7

Help your learner

In this unit, learners will practise making relevant observations (Sections 5.1, 5.4 and 5.5), making predictions of what will happen based on scientific knowledge and understanding, and suggesting how to test these (Section 5.4). They will also practise using observation to test predictions (Section 5.1). To help them:

1 Do some of the investigations with learners. Ask them to predict what will happen and then test their predictions by observing what happens.

2 Find things at home that are opaque, transparent or translucent. Get learners to identify them and tell you why they are made of these materials.

TEACHING TIP

Remind learners that they must *never* look directly at the Sun.

5.1 Light travels in straight lines

blocking, shadows

Understanding shadows

Ahmad and Umar are playing outside in the sunshine. Ahmad has his arms stretched out. Umar has his hands behind his back.

1. What is the light source?

_____

2. Ahmad and Umar are **blocking** the light source, so **shadows** form.

   a Whose shadow is drawn on the wrong side – Ahmad's or Umar's?

_____

b Explain your answer by filling in the blanks in these sentences. Choose from the words in the box. You may need to use some words more than once.

| Umar's   blocked   straight   Ahmad's   solid |

A shadow forms when light is _____ by a _____ object. Light travels in _____ lines, so _____ shadow is drawn in the right place. Because light travels in _____ lines, it cannot go around an object, so _____ shadow is drawn on the wrong side.

3 a Choose an object outside, such as a tree or a building. Predict where its shadow will fall in the morning.

_____

b Give a reason for your prediction.

_____

_____

c Test your prediction.

CHECK YOUR LEARNING

◯ I know that light travels in straight lines.

◯ I know that shadows form when light is blocked by a solid object.

◯ I can predict where a shadow falls and test my prediction.

5 Shadows   45

5.2 Which materials let light through?

opaque, translucent, transparent

Identify opaque, transparent and translucent materials

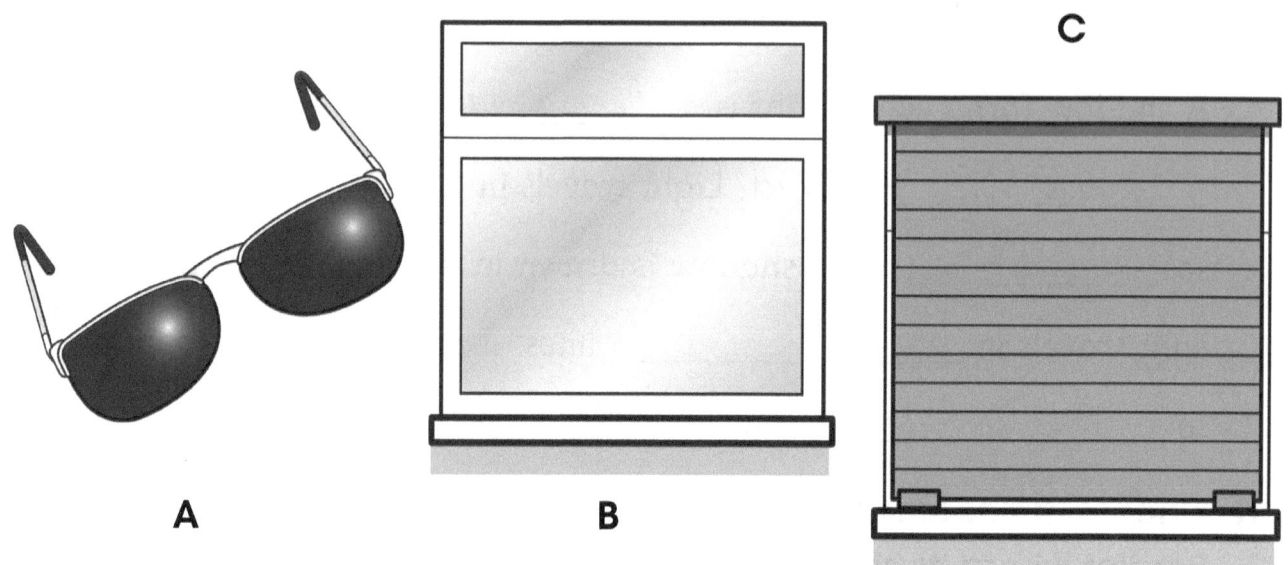

A   B   C

1 a Which of the objects is made of **opaque** material?
_____

b What tells you this?
_____

c Why is this object made of opaque material?
_____

2 a Which of the objects is made of **translucent** material?
_____

b What tells you this?
_____

c Why is this object made of translucent material?
_____

3 a Which of the objects is made of **transparent** material?

_____

b What tells you this?

_____

c Why is this object made of transparent material?

_____

Think about it!

4 Why do you think bathroom windows are made of translucent glass?

_____

_____

> **KEY FACT**
>
> You can use shadow shades to decide which materials are opaque (the darkest shade) and which are transparent (the lightest shade). The translucent materials are all the shades in between.

CHECK YOUR LEARNING

◯ I know that opaque, translucent and transparent materials let through different amounts of light.

◯ I can apply this knowledge to explain why objects are made of these different materials.

5.3 Silhouettes and shadow puppets

silhouette

Explain how a shadow puppet works

Harris and Henry have made a shadow puppet of a dragon. They have a strong lamp and they are looking at the shadow on a white wall.

1 What are Harris and Henry using as a light source?

_____

Remember:

Light will travel in a straight line from a light source to the puppet.

2 What are they using for a screen? Explain why they have chosen this.

_____

_____

_____

3 Why does the puppet form a shadow on the wall?

_____

_____

_____

4 Why can you describe a shadow puppet as a **silhouette**?

_____

_____

_____

_____

CHECK YOUR LEARNING

○ I know how a shadow puppet works.

5.4 What affects the size of a shadow?

Make a shadow puppet bigger

1 Harris and Henry want to make the shadow of the dragon bigger on the wall. Predict whether they must move the puppet closer to the lamp or closer to the wall.

_____

2 Test your prediction using a lamp, a solid object and a wall.

3 Draw a diagram to show your answer. Include the light from the lamp, an outline to represent the object and a line to show the wall. Draw the object in two places – one closer to the lamp and one closer to the wall to show the difference in the size of the shadow.

CHECK YOUR LEARNING

○ I know that the size of the shadow is affected by the position of an object.

○ I can draw a diagram to explain my answer.

5.5 Investigating shadow lengths

Analyse the results of a shadow stick experiment

The drawing shows the results of a shadow stick experiment.

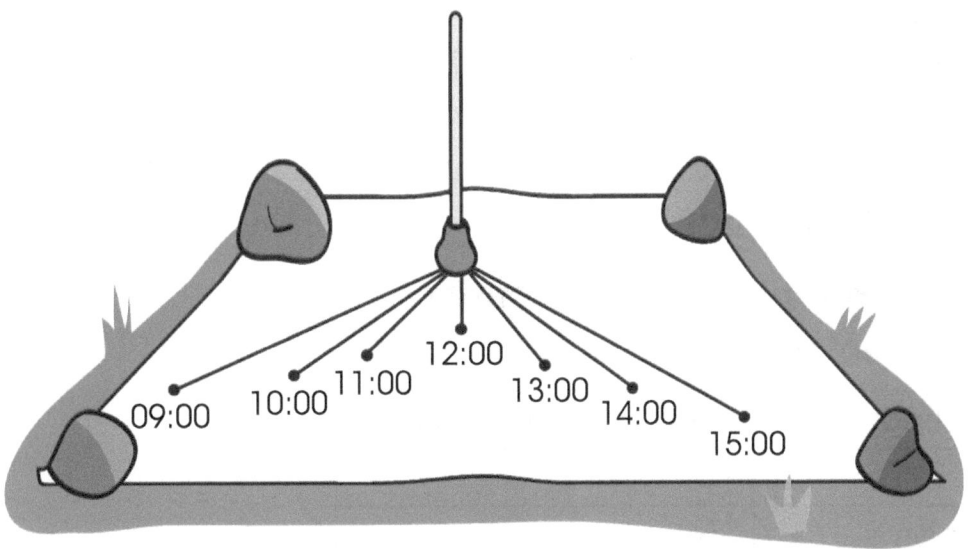

1 a At what time on the shadow stick is the Sun highest in the sky?

_____

b Does this result in a long or a short shadow?

_____

2 a At which times on the shadow stick is the Sun lowest in the sky?

_____

b Does this result in a long or a short shadow?

_____

CHECK YOUR LEARNING

◯ I know that shadows change in length and position throughout the day.

◯ I can analyse data on a diagram.

5.6 Measuring light intensity

light intensity

Measuring light intensity in a building

When designing a building, architects think about how much light is needed in different parts of it. This depends on what the area will be used for. For example, you need a more brightly lit area to do needlework than you do when you walk down a corridor.

> **KEY FACT**
>
> **Light intensity** changes at different times of the day. Light intensity is measured in units of 'lux' by a light meter.

Here are some examples of light intensity needed in different parts of a school building.

Part of building	Light intensity (in lux)
corridors	100
changing rooms	150
assembly hall	300
computer room	500

1 What is light intensity?

_____

2 What instrument can you use to measure light intensity?

_____

3 Suggest the light intensity in lux needed for these areas of a school.

   a Outside parking area _____

   b Classroom _____

CHECK YOUR LEARNING

○ I know what light intensity is.

○ I can suggest levels of light intensity for parts of a building.

6 Earth's movements

What learners will practise and reinforce

The activities in this Skills Builder unit give learners further practice in the following topics in the Learner's Book and Activity Book:

Topic	In this topic, learners will:
6.1 The Sun, the Earth and the Moon	discover that the Earth moves around the Sun and the Moon moves around the Earth in orbits
6.2 Does the Sun move?	understand that the Sun does not really move even though it appears to
6.3 The Earth rotates on its axis	explain how the Earth rotates on its axis
6.4 Sunrise and sunset	see Challenge, Section 6.4
6.5 The Earth revolves around the Sun	use a diagram to explain what causes the seasons
6.6 Exploring the solar system	discover what scientists have found out about Mars
6.7 Exploring the stars	see Challenge, Section 6.7

Help your learner

In this unit, learners will practise making relevant observations (Sections 6.3 and 6.5) and making predictions of what will happen and suggesting and communicating how to test these predictions (Sections 6.2, 6.3 and 6.6). To help them:

1 Explain to learners that the Moon is still in the sky during the day. Guide them in observing that the Moon is in different parts of the sky from one day to the next because it orbits the Earth once every 30 days.

2 Help learners observe how the Sun appears to move across the sky.

6.1 The Sun, the Earth and the Moon

orbit, planet, star

Analyse a diagram of the Sun, Earth and Moon

1 Complete the table by filling in the letters from the diagram in the second column. You will need to use some letters more than once. The first one is done for you as an example.

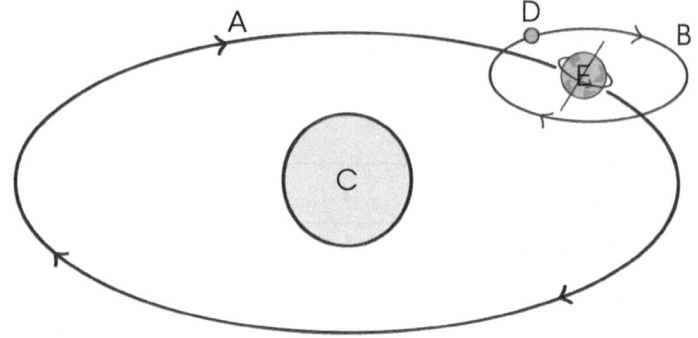

	Letter on diagram
Moon	D
Sun	
Earth	
orbit of the Moon around the Earth	
orbit of the Earth around the Sun	
a **planet**	
a **star**	
a body in space that gives out light	
a body in space that reflects light	

CHECK YOUR LEARNING

◯ I know that the Earth moves around the Sun and the Moon moves around the Earth in orbits.

◯ I know the difference between stars and planets.

6.2 Does the Sun move?

apparent

Show the apparent movement of the Sun on a shadow stick drawing

Here is a picture of a shadow stick experiment. Look at the position of the Sun at 09:00. A sunbeam comes from the Sun (s) and casts a shadow of the stick, labelled 09:00.

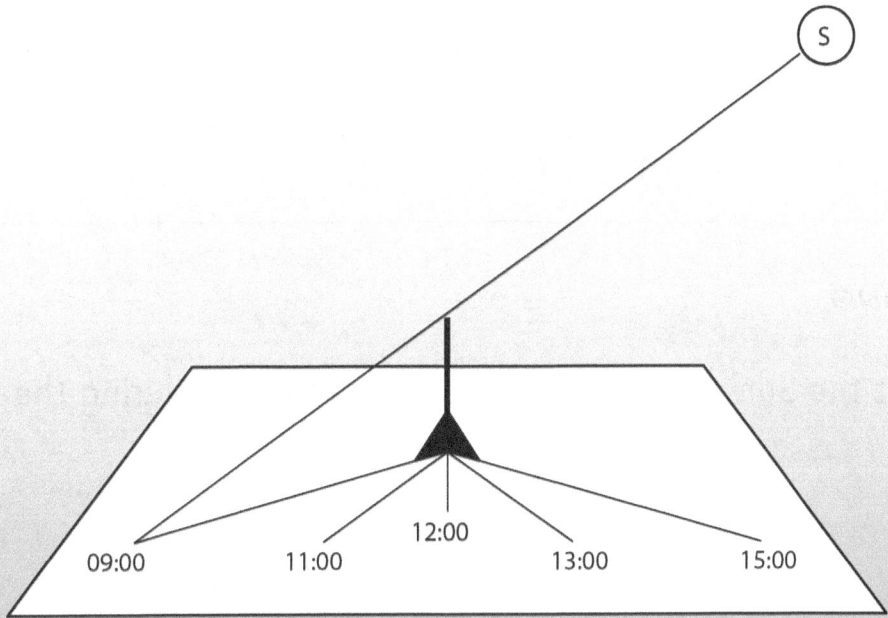

Remember:

Look back at Unit 5 to remind yourself of the shadow stick experiment.

1 On the picture, draw sunbeams and suns for the shadows at 11:00, 12:00, 13:00 and 15:00.

2 What does the Sun appear to do between 09:00 and 15:00?

_____

_____

3 Does the Sun really do what it appears to do? Explain your answer using your scientific knowledge.

_____

_____

_____

CHECK YOUR LEARNING

○ I can show that the Sun appears to move across the sky during the day.

6.3 The Earth rotates on its axis

axis, rotation

Complete a diagram of the movement of the Earth

Look at this diagram of the Earth.

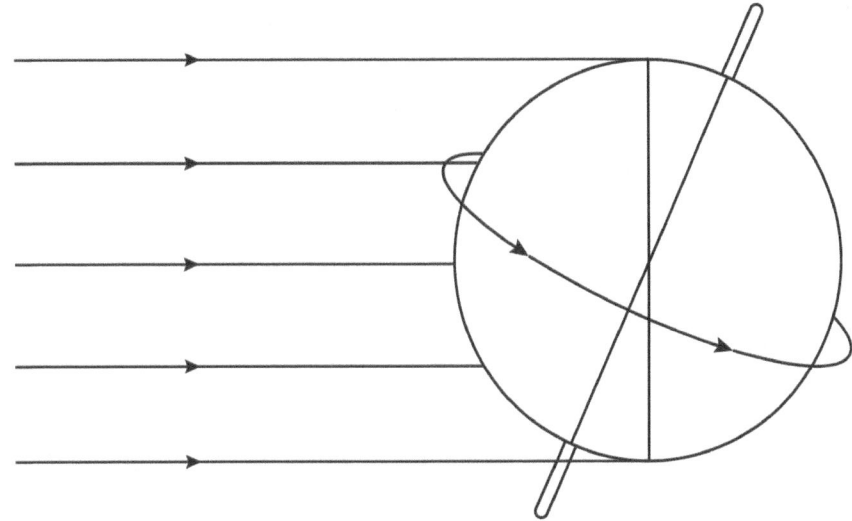

1 On the diagram, label the Sun's rays and the Earth's **axis** and **rotation**.

2 How long does one complete rotation take?

_____

3 Why does everywhere on the Earth's surface have some hours of daylight and some hours of darkness every day?

_____

_____

4 On the diagram, shade the part of the Earth having night.

CHECK YOUR LEARNING

○ I can label a diagram of the Earth.

○ I understand why places on Earth experience day and night.

6.5 The Earth revolves around the Sun

Analyse a diagram of Earth revolving around the Sun

Look at this diagram. It shows Earth in one of its positions as it revolves around the Sun.

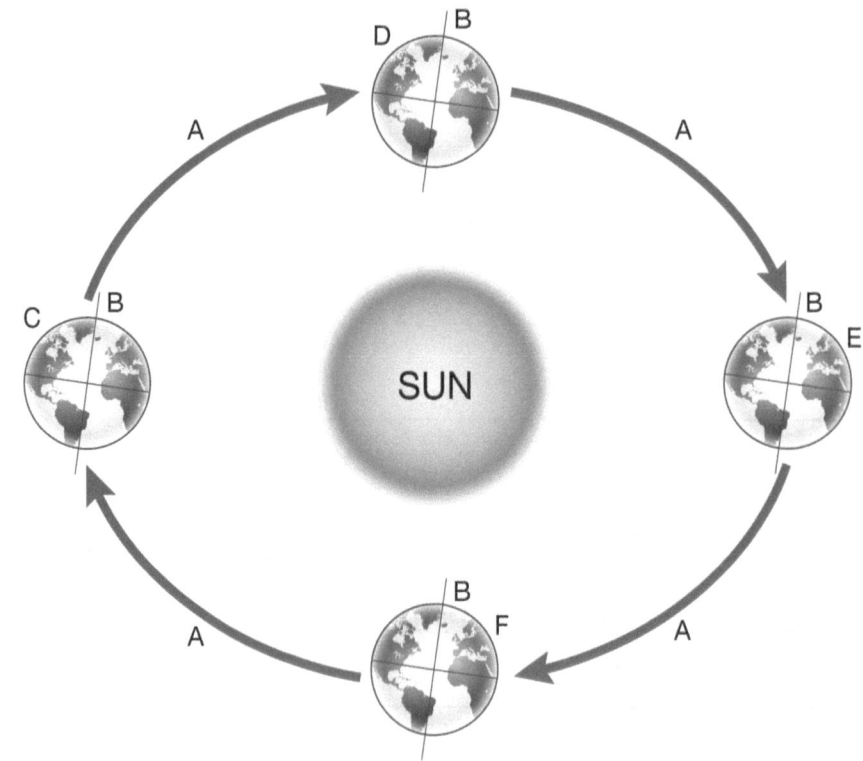

1 a Name the path (A) Earth takes when it revolves around the Sun.

_____

b What is one complete movement of Earth around the Sun called?

_____

c What length of time does one complete movement take?

_____

2 a What are the imaginary lines labelled B?

_____

b What movement does the Earth make around this imaginary line?

_____

c Does this movement and the movement you named in 1b take place at the same time?

_____

3 It is June when Earth is in position C and September when Earth is in position D. What months are they when Earth is in positions E and F?

E is _____

F is _____

4 Where you live, in which of Earth's positions (C, D, E or F) do you have the longest days?

_____

5 Think about it!

Why do you have longest days during the month you named in Question 4? Look at the diagram for clues.

_____

_____

CHECK YOUR LEARNING

◯ I can understand a diagram of Earth revolving around the Sun.

6.6 Exploring the solar system

> atmosphere, carbon dioxide, astronauts

Learn about Mars

Mars is often called the 'Red Planet' because it looks red in the sky. The ancient Greeks and Romans called it Mars, after the god of war. They associated war with the colour red. For a long time, this was all people knew about Mars.

In the 17th century, the telescope was invented. This made it possible for scientists to find out more about Mars. In 1666, the Italian scientist Giovanni Cassini observed that Mars rotates on its axis once every 24 hours and 40 minutes. By 1700, scientists had seen ice on Mars and suggested that people could be living there! They called the people Martians.

During the 1800s, telescopes improved a lot so scientists were able to see more. They discovered that Mars has two moons, which they called Phobos and Deimos. Scientists could see straight lines on Mars linking green areas. They suggested that the straight lines were canals that the Martians had built to water their crops!

1 a Before telescopes were invented, in what ways did people study Mars?

_____

  b What did they know about Mars in ancient Roman times?

_____

2 As telescopes improved, scientists discovered more. Name two things they observed that are true.

_____

_____

3 Why did scientists think there could be people living on Mars?

_____

The 20th and 21st centuries

Over the past 50 years, many spacecraft have visited Mars and taken photographs. Recently 'Rovers' have landed on Mars and sent back detailed information to Earth about the rocks, the ice and the atmosphere. We now know that the red colour noticed by the ancient Romans is due to iron oxide in the rocks.

Scientists know from samples of the **atmosphere** round Mars that it consists mostly of **carbon dioxide**.

6 Earth's movements

They have studied many photographs of dry valleys on the surface of Mars. These could have been caused by water in the past. But there is no water on the surface now, only some ice at the poles.

By 2020, scientists want to have a science laboratory permanently on Mars where **astronauts** can visit by spacecraft.

4 Why have scientists discovered so much more about Mars in the last 50 years?

_____

_____

5 Give two reasons why humans could not survive on Mars.

_____

_____

CHECK YOUR LEARNING

◯ I can read and understand a case study about Mars.

◯ I can understand how scientists have managed to find out more about Mars over the years.

Answers

1 Investigating plant growth

1.3

Draw a chart of seed germination

1

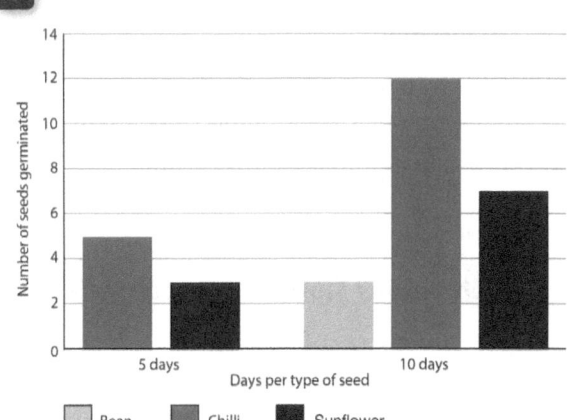

2 a Seeds do not need light to germinate. Ella planted the seeds in soil so they did not get light but they still germinated.
   b They put seeds in warm place and watered them.

3 The chilli seeds.

4 The bean seeds.

5 The bigger the seed, the longer it takes to germinate.

1.4

Identify the things that plants need to grow

1 a We call the things that plants need to grow <u>factors</u>.
   b Plants need <u>light</u> so they can make food to help them grow.
   c Plants need <u>water</u> to give them strong stems and firm leaves.
   d Plants need <u>warmth</u>, but they grow best when it is not too cold or too hot.
   e Plants need <u>air</u> because they are living things.

2 **Think about it!**
Plants use light to make food in their leaves. Seeds have a food store that they use to germinate so they do not need light to make food.

2 The life cycle of flowering plants

2.1

Draw a bar chart of different flowers

1

Type of flower	Number observed
big	10
small	16
scented	5
no scent	9

2

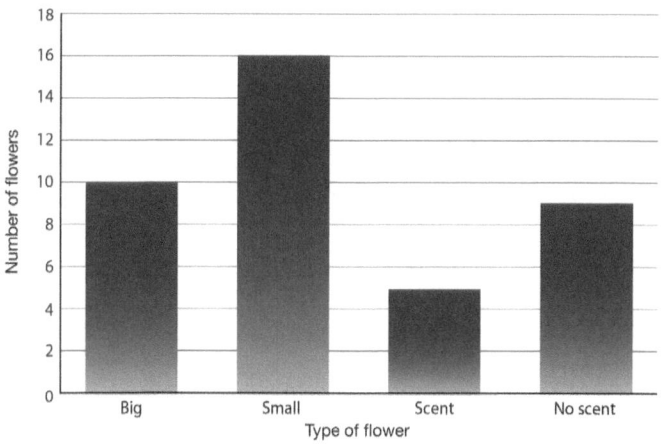

3 Flowers form the seeds that grow into new plants.

2.2

Explain how seeds suit the way they are spread

1 by water = seed has spongy covering that helps it float

by air = seed is very light with thin, papery wings

by animals = seed has spines and hooks

by gravity = fruit is heavy and drops to the ground

by explosion = seed pods dry out and burst open

2 Seed dispersal.

3 So they grow away from the parent plant and have enough space, light and water to grow into new plants.

2.4

Identify and describe parts of a flower

1

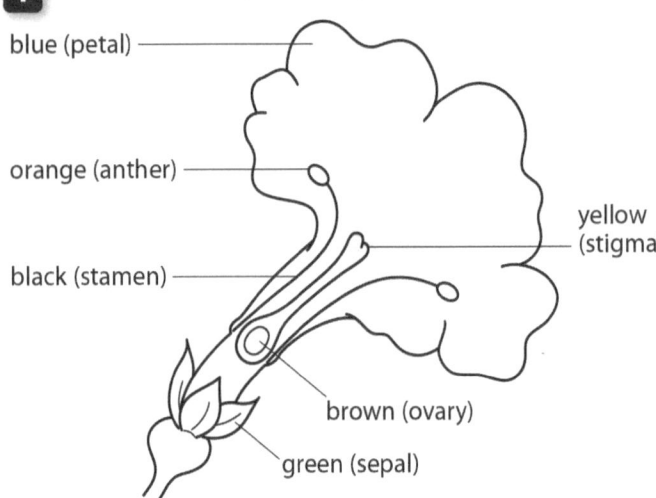

blue (petal)
orange (anther)
black (stamen)
yellow (stigma)
brown (ovary)
green (sepal)

2 The <u>sepals</u> are little green leaves that protect the flower bud. The <u>petals</u> often have bright colours to attract insects. The male parts of the flower are the <u>stamens</u>. They make pollen in their tips, called <u>anthers</u>. The female part of the flower is made up of the <u>stigma</u>, which collects pollen, and the <u>ovary</u>, which contains the eggs.

2.5

Answer questions about pollination and fertilisation

1 **b** pollination.

2 **b** bright colours.

3 **d** fertilisation.

4 **a** ovary.

5 **Think about it!**

A pollinator will visit the male flower and collect pollen. It will then move to the female flower and leave pollen on the stigma.

2.6

Identify which colour flowers insects visit most

1

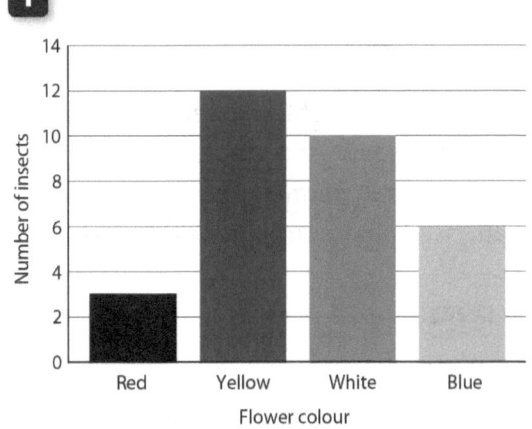

2 **a** Yellow.

b Red. Insects do not see red very well – they see colours such as white and yellow best.

3 **a** Insects visit yellow flowers most/red flowers least.

b Repeat the investigation a few times.

2.7

Complete a crossword puzzle

Across
3 fertilisation
5 seeds
8 anthers
9 pollination
10 growth

Down
1 flowering
2 germination
4 fruit
6 dispersal
7 pollinator

3 States of matter

3.1

Evaporation true or false

1. Evaporation occurs when a liquid changes to a gas. ✓
2. Heat makes evaporation happen faster. ✓
3. Particles of a liquid must lose energy before they can evaporate. ✗
4. Evaporation makes wet clothes dry. ✓
5. Water disappears when it evaporates. ✗

3.2

Explain how evaporation dries things

1. Kumei can use a hairdryer to dry the dress. (A fan will take too long because they only have ten minutes before they leave for the party.)
2. The particles of water on the dress will heat up until they have enough energy to change into water vapour. The gas will escape from the surface of the dress, making the dress dry.
3. Heat and moving air.
4. Evaporation is useful for drying foods such fish or fruit. It also keeps us cool by sweating.

3.3

Draw a graph of factors that affect evaporation

1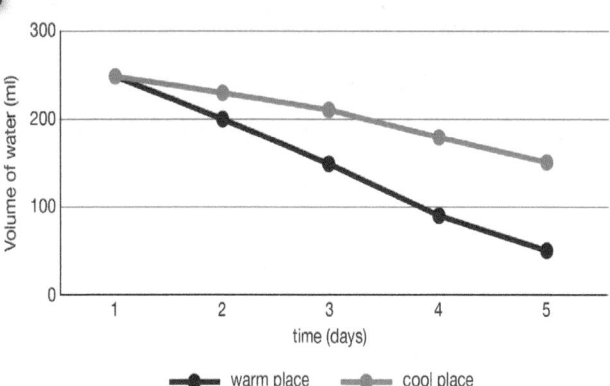

2 a The bowl in the warm place. There was less water in the bowl in the warm place at the end of the investigation than the bowl in the cool place.
  b Temperature.

3 Yes. The bowls were the same and had the same amount of water in them at the start of the investigation. The only factor that changed was the place where the bowls were put.

3.4

Solutions true or false

1. A solution is made of a solute and solvent. ✓
2. The solvent dissolves in the solute to form a solution. ✗
3. We cannot see the solute particles in a solution. ✓
4. We can separate the solute and solvent in a solution by evaporation. ✓
5. The water that evaporates from a salt solution will taste salty. ✗

3.5

Complete sentences about condensation

1. Condensation happens when a <u>gas</u> changes to a <u>liquid</u>.
2. We know that condensation has happened when we see <u>drops</u> of water on a surface.
3. Condensation happens when water vapour touches a <u>cooler</u> surface. This makes the particles of water vapour <u>cool down</u> and <u>lose</u> energy.
4. The opposite process to condensation is <u>evaporation</u>.

3.6

Explain the water cycle

1. a Evaporation.
   b B (the Sun).
   c To heat the particles of water so they gain enough energy to break free from the surface of the water and evaporate.
2. a Cloud.
   b Condensation; part C.
   c Condensation happens when the particles of a gas lose energy. This makes the gas cool and change to a liquid.
3. a Water/rain.
   b Liquid.
   c Solid/snow; part F.
4. **Think about it!**
   Antarctica is the coldest place on Earth. It is too cold for water to evaporate so no clouds form. This means that it cannot rain there.

3.8

Melting multiple choice

1. b melting.
2. c solid + heat → liquid.
3. a liquid − heat → solid.
4. a their particles gain energy and break away from the solid.
5. d freezing.

3.9

Measuring temperature with a thermometer

1. a Always hold the <u>top</u> of the thermometer.
   b Make sure your eye is <u>level with</u> the top of the liquid in the thermometer.
   c When you measure the temperature of liquids, make sure <u>all</u> of the bulb is in the liquid.
   d Read the temperature scale <u>after</u> the thermometer reading stops changing.
   e Read the temperature scale <u>before</u> you take the thermometer out of the liquid.
2. a 25 °C.
   b There should be lines marking 100 °C (boiling point of water) and c 0 °C (melting point of ice).

4 The way we see things

4.1

Describe how we see objects

1. Lamp.
2. Needle and thread/sewing.
3. There should be a straight line from the lamp to the needle and thread, with an arrow pointing to the needle and thread. There should be a second line from the needle and thread to Mrs Liong's eyes, with the arrow pointing to her eyes.
4. The Sun.

4.3

Explain how to use a mirror to see behind you

1. Adeline is looking at a <u>mirror</u>. She can see the <u>image</u> of her face. This is because the <u>mirror</u> has a smooth, shiny <u>surface</u>. It <u>reflects</u> light well. Thandi is holding a second <u>mirror</u>. Adeline can see the <u>image</u> of the back of her head in the mirror <u>in front</u> of her.

2. There should be a straight line from the lamp to the back of Adeline's head, labelled 'light from source'. There should be straight lines from the back of Adeline's head to the mirror Thandi is holding, then from the mirror Thandi is holding to the mirror in front of Adeline, then from the mirror in front of Adeline into Adeline's eyes.

3. **Think about it!**
   The Sun is the most likely natural light source, or perhaps firelight. Artificial light sources could be electric light, paraffin lamp, gas lamp.

4.4

Compare how well two surfaces reflect light

1. Learner's own response.

2. Learners should predict that shiny, metal objects like a saucepan lid, an aluminium foil container or a glass will reflect light well and that wooden or stone surfaces will absorb light. To make the test fair, they should shine the same torch on each surface for the same length of time. They should place the surface being tested in the same position each time.

3. Learner's own response.

4. Conclusion is that smooth shiny surfaces such as metal reflect light well. Surfaces such as wood do not reflect any light, they absorb light.

5. Repeat the experiment using different materials.

5 Shadows

5.1

Understanding shadows

1. The Sun.

2. a Umar's.
   b A shadow forms when light is <u>blocked</u> by a <u>solid</u> object. Light travels in <u>straight</u> lines, so <u>Ahmad's</u> shadow is drawn in the right place. Because light travels in <u>straight</u> lines, it cannot go around an object, so <u>Umar's</u> shadow is drawn on the wrong side.

3. a Learner chooses an object and predicts where its shadow will fall.
   b If the Sun is behind the object, the shadow will be in front of the object, because the object is blocking the light that falls behind it. If the Sun is in front of the object, the shadow will be behind the object, because the object is blocking the light that falls in front of it.
   c Learner tests their prediction.

5.2

Identify opaque, transparent and translucent materials

1. a C.
   b It does not let any light through.
   c Shutters are used to block out the Sun and keep the inside of a room in shade.

2. a A.
   b They let some but not all the light through.
   c Sunglasses must block out some sunlight but not all of it, otherwise you would not be able to see.

3. a B.
   b It lets all the light through.
   c Windows must be transparent to allow all the light in.

4. **Think about it!**
   So that they let in light, but people cannot see into the bathroom.

5.3

Explain how a shadow puppet works

1 A lamp.

2 A white wall. They have chosen this so the shadow will show up well.

3 The puppet blocks the light from the lamp and the shadow of the puppet is projected onto the wall.

4 A silhouette is a solid image of a person or scene that does not let light through. A shadow puppet is the same thing, but it is used to project onto a screen.

5.4

Make a shadow puppet bigger

1 They will need to move the puppet closer to the lamp to make the shadow bigger.

2 Learners should test their prediction.

3

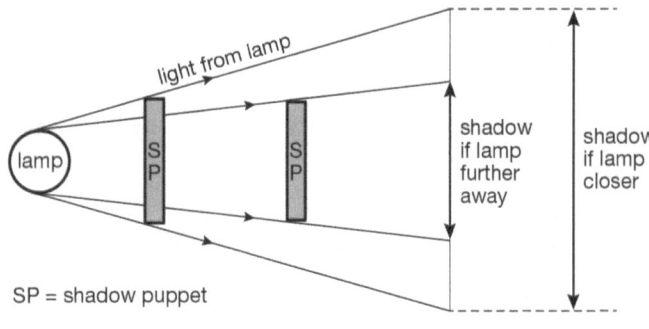

SP = shadow puppet

5.5

Analyse the results of a shadow stick experiment

1 a 12:00.
b Short.

2 a 09:00 and 15:00.
b Long.

5.6

Measure light intensity in a building

1 The amount of light in an area.

2 Light meter.

3 a 50 lux (answers may vary).
b 400–600 lux (answers may vary).

6 Earth's movements

6.1

Analyse a diagram of the Sun, Earth and Moon

1

	Letter on diagram
Moon	D
Sun	C
Earth	E
orbit of the Moon around the Earth	B
orbit of the Earth around the Sun	A
a planet	E
a star	C
a body in space that gives out light	C
a body in space that reflects light	E

6.2

Show the apparent movement of the Sun on a shadow stick drawing

1

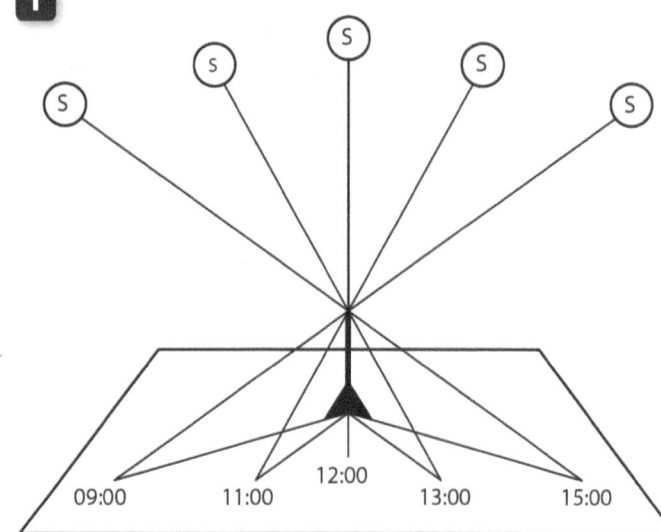

2 It appears to move across the sky.

3 No. The Sun only *appears* to be moving. It is actually the Earth that is moving.

6.3

Complete a diagram of movement of the Earth

1 and **4**

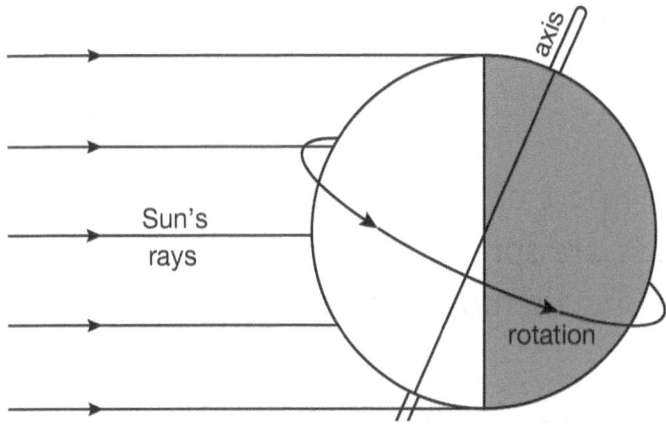

2 24 hours.

3 The Earth makes one complete rotation every 24 hours, so for part of the time a place is facing the Sun and part of the time it is facing away from the Sun and having night.

6.5

Analyse a diagram of Earth revolving around the Sun

1 a Orbit.
　　b Revolution.
　　c 365¼ days.

2 a Earth's axis.
　　b Rotation.
　　c Yes.

3 E is December, F is March.

4 Answer C if you live in the northern hemisphere and E if you live in the southern hemisphere.

5 Think about it!
During the month with the longest days, the particular hemisphere is tilted towards the Sun.

6.6

Learn about Mars

1 a They looked at Mars in the night sky with the naked eye.
　　b It was red.

2 Mars rotates on its axis once every 24 hours and 40 minutes. Mars has two moons, Phobos and Deimos.

3 They thought there was water on Mars. They thought people had built canals on Mars.

4 Spacecraft have flown past Mars and taken many photographs. Rovers have landed on Mars and brought back samples of rock and air.

5 There is no water or oxygen.

Glossary

1 Investigating plant growth

factors	things that have an effect on other things
germinate	when a seed starts to grow
seeds	the part of a plant that can grow into a new plant

2 The life cycle of flowering plants

anther	the tip of the male part of a flower
dispersal	the way that seeds are spread around
fertilisation	the process that joins the pollen and eggs to make seeds
ovary	the part of a plant that contains eggs
petals	the parts of the flower that are often brightly coloured
pollen	a yellow or brown powder made in the stamen
pollination	the process that brings pollen from the stamen to the stigma of a flower
pollinator	an insect that pollinates flowers
scent	the smell of flower petals
sepals	an outer ring of small green leaves on the base of a flower
stamen	the male part of a flower
stigma	the tip of the female parts of a flower
style	a hollow tube that connects the stigma and the ovary in a flower

3 States of matter

condensation	when a gas changes to a liquid
contracts	gets smaller
evaporation	when a liquid turns into a gas
expands	gets bigger

factors	variables in an investigation or experiment
melting	the process by which a solid changes to a liquid
melting point	the temperature at which a solid melts
particles	very small parts of something
solutions	mixtures of one substance with another, where the dissolved substance can no longer be seen
temperature	a measurement of how hot or cold something is
thermometers	instruments used to measure temperature
water cycle	when water evaporates from seas, rivers and lakes, condenses to form clouds and falls back to Earth as rain
water vapour	the gas formed when liquid water changes into a gas

4 The way we see things

absorb	to take in a substance
image	the picture of the object that you see on a screen or in a mirror
light source	a place where light comes from, for example the Sun or a torch
mirror	a very smooth, shiny surface that reflects light well
object	the thing that is reflected
reflects	bounces off a surface
surface	the top layer that is next to the air

5 Shadows

blocking	stopping something from continuing on its way
light intensity	the amount of light in an area
opaque	does not allow light to pass through
shadows	shapes formed when light is blocked by some types of solid object
silhouette	the shadow that forms when you hold an opaque object in front of a light source

translucent	allows some of the light to pass through
transparent	allows all the light to pass through

6 Earth's movements

apparent	when it looks as though something has caused an action but in fact it was caused by something else
astronauts	people who travel in space
atmosphere	the layer of gases that surrounds the Earth
axis	an imaginary line passing through Earth from the North Pole to the South pole; Earth rotates around this axis
carbon dioxide	a gas that humans and animals breathe out and plants take in
orbit	the path taken by a body moving around a larger body in space
planet	a body in space that orbits a star and reflects light from the star
rotation	the movement of a body around its own axis
star	a body in space that gives off light and heat

Remember:

Use these words when you discuss the topics in the unit so that learners become familiar with them.